WOLVES

WOLVES

PATRICK HOOK

GRAMERCY BOOKS
NEW YORK

First published in 1998 by
PRC Publishing Ltd,
Kiln House, 210 New Kings Road, London SW6 4NZ

This edition is published by Gramercy Books,®
a division of Random House Value Publishing, Inc.,
201 East 50th Street, New York, New York, 10022.

Gramercy Books® and design are registered trademarks of
Random House Value Publishing, Inc.

Random House
New York • Toronto • London • Sydney • Auckland
http://www.randomhouse.com/

Printed and bound in Singapore

A CIP catalogue record for this book is available from the Library of Congress.

ISBN 0-517-16082-X

8 7 6 5 4 3 2 1

Contents

PREFACE

Wolves

This book, as its title suggests, is about the wolf. It attempts to tell the story about where the wolf came from, its status today, and what future there is for it. In doing so, the book will cover the different types of wolves, which of them are true members of the family, and which are not. It also examines the long-standing interaction between man and the wolf. From the very dawn of time, wolves have been the stuff of myth and legend, we will therefore look at this as well.

I have been fascinated by wolves for most of my life, and, although I have worked in motor-racing for a large part of it, I have also worked as an animal handler and trainer. During this time I have belonged to various organisations and societies dedicated to the study of wildlife, and have tried to do my "bit" to further the cause of conservation. Whilst compiling this book, my research led me to discover over and over again the consistency of two things: the affection wolves have for each other, and the cruelty they have suffered at the hands of mankind.

Things are changing, however, and if one looks at the massive swing in attitudes over the last 30 years, there is real hope. At this stage I would like to pay tribute to those whose dedication in studying and conserving the wolf make this hope realistic. The more of us that show our support for conservation generally, the less power the vested interests (against conservation) will have. These are often fighting against things they little understand—many times backed only by ignorance, myth, legend, and bigotry.

It pays to remember that the only way to make significant change is at the political level, with governments. It also pays to remember that there is only one thing that a government is interested in ultimately, and that is staying in power. If we, the voters, can demonstrate that helping to save the environment and all that is in it, will do them good—we will see results. If not, we will hear promises, platitudes, and hot air. I leave it up to you, the reader, to decide who to believe, and who to vote for!

Patrick Hook, Exeter, March 1998

Right: Wolves evolved at about the same time as their major predator —humans. It is up to the predator to turn protector if wolves are to survive in any numbers in the wild.

EVOLUTION & HISTORY

Wolves

About 100 million years ago there was a group of animals called the creodonts. It was from these that the direct lineage of the wolf began, during the Palaeocene epoch, about 60 million years ago. At this time dogs and cats had not separated out into distinct families, and were in fact represented by an animal called miacis, which was like a long-legged weasel. It was from this that all the canids descended—these are the dog-like animals, which include the wolves. Over the next 40 million years the felines and the canids became more and more different, until during the Miocene period they had evolved into quite distinct animals.

Wolves evolved first about a million years ago as descendants of animals from the Asiatic continent. This was during the last great Ice Age, which ended about 10,000 years ago. They have since split into various sub-species, and spread throughout Asia and Europe, and into America across the Bering land bridge.

During the late Pleistocene period, there were three true wolves in North America—the gray wolf, the red wolf, and the dire wolf, which has since become extinct. Asiatic and American wolves have not been able to become distinct species because of the link between the two continents each time the Bering land bridge was re-established. Every time this happened it ensured a fresh genetic influx, which has had a major influence on how wolves have evolved. Without the link we would probably have rather different animals in America today.

Wolves and humans evolved during more or less the same period. While this was far too long ago for recorded history, it is believed that archaeological evidence points to a mutual coexistence of respect and tolerance while both were hunters. It all changed once humans started to live as farmers, because it meant that they started to keep livestock. Immediately this set humans and wolves against each other, especially when times were hard.

Wolves

While the necessity to keep wolves away from farmland was often the initial reason for hunting them, it is also undoubtedly true that the human love of killing things for sport had its part to play in the decline in wolf numbers. Sadly, this is still true today, with many reintroduced wolves being shot or trapped by modern-day huntsmen.

In reality, the cost of wolf predations to farmers is small, with bad husbandry accounting for far more losses than wolves. Unfortunately many wild claims are made against them—when in fact the cost of livestock killed or injured by domestic dogs regularly outstrips that of wolves. It has been estimated that in 1997 wolves in the Northern Rockies killed domestic animals with a market value of just over $30,000, of which reintroduced Yellowstone wolves accounted for approximately half the total. This was made up of five cattle, 80 sheep and one dog. There have been many deaths of dogs in this area, most of which have been hounds that had inadvertently run into wolf packs, but put altogether, this is hardly high level damage. On top of this, while wolves attacking and killing humans have been the subjects of countless legends and fairy tales, there appear to be no documented cases of it ever happening in North America. The main cause of antagonism between man and wolves has been that of competition for food, especially when farm livestock has been involved. These days little excuse seems to be necessary for humans to hunt and kill wolves. Any advantage they had in primeval times went with the invention of the snare. Today the chances of wolves evading persecution have gone even further with hunters using high-power weapons from aircraft.

Man's deep loathing for the wolf is of long standing. On the side of the wolves we have the maternal instincts exhibited by she-wolves who have, it is said, suckled many famous people, from Rome's founders Romulus and Remus to the German hero Siegfried, the Persian seer Zoroaster, and the Turkish leader Tu Kueh. Ranged against this we have writers from antiquity onward—the Greek Aesop used the wolf as the instrument of evil in his fables; in the Aeneid, the Roman poet Virgil writes:

"So seizes the grim wolf the tender lamb,
In vain lamented by the bleating dam."

Biblically, in both Old and New Testaments, the wolf is used as the indicator of evil—indeed, the Christian faith would base much of its religious imagery on the flock of believers, sheep succoured by Christ the Good Shepherd, against the Devil and his wolfish cohorts. This fear was multiplied during the credulous Middle Ages when fear of witchcraft would lead to stories of lycanthropy and fear of werewolves. These fears were very real—in France, between 1520 and 1630, over 30,000 people were tortured and burned for being suspected werewolves.

As well as fear of werewolves and the protection of livestock, there is also the fear of personal attack. An example of the stories of wolf attacks on humans is that of the eighteenth century "Beast of Gevaudan," which, as we will see later, may not have been a wolf after all. The story has shaped much of modern myth and legend about wolves. It all happened in south-central France, where, between 1764 and 1767, up to a hundred people were killed by a beast described as "a cow-sized, wolf-like monster." Most of these

Wolves

victims were small children. Some accounts maintain that there were two or more beasts responsible for the deaths, although most indicate only one. It was known as the *Anthropophage du Gevaudan*, which translates as the "Man Eating Beast of Gevaudan."

In June 1764 a young woman was attacked by the beast, which it is believed was the first assault on a human. She survived—one of a lucky few. She was out tending her family's herd of cattle in the Forêt de Mercoire, when a great wolf-like animal loped out of the forest. Her dogs ran away, but her cattle charged at it instead. It was undeterred, but eventually the cattle drove it away.

The beast was found and shot by two hunters, who hit it four times at close range, but it was not killed. It was further wounded when a Captain Du Hamel, together with 60 men, hunted and shot at it several times. Another attempt to hunt the beast down was made when an experienced wolf-hunter named Denneval was sent by King Louis XV himself to kill it. Before Denneval got there, three brothers of the de la Chaumette family shot the beast twice, again without killing it. Denneval was unsuccessful, and gave up in June 1765. King Louis XV sent his chief gun-carrier—Antoine de Beauterne; he had more luck, succeeding in killing a particularly large wolf on September 21, 1765. This wolf was six feet long, and was preserved until this century in the Museum of Natural History in Paris.

Sadly for the populace of the region, however, the killings continued. Many of the locals considered that they were being punished by God for their sins, and made pilgrimages to Notre-Dame de Beaulieu Cathedral near Mount Chauvet to pray for deliverance. Others believed that the beast was a *loup-garou*, or werewolf. One of the peasants who went to the cathedral was a hermit by the name of Jean Chastel. While he was there, he had his rifle and three bullets blessed. Later, while participating in a large hunt, he shot and killed the beast at Sogne d'Aubert.

The important question as far as the credibility of wolves is concerned is, "Was it a wolf or not?" At the time some learned people thought it might have been a wolverine. Others said it was a new species, made by crossing a tiger and a hyena. Other opinions were that it was a bear, or even a baboon. The carcass of Chastel's kill was discovered earlier this century in the basement of the Museum of Natural History in Paris, where it was identified as a wolf, and discarded due to its poor condition. It was later re-discovered by a zoologist called Franz Jullien, who identified it as a striped hyena (*Hyena hyena*). What it was doing in southern France can only be guessed at, as it is a native of the African continent.

There are other supposed attacks on man by wolves, one of which was claimed to have happened in Russia in 1875, when 161 people were "killed and eaten by wolves." Another report came from north-west Turkey in 1968, when two villagers were supposedly killed and eaten. It is difficult to authenticate either of these stories, especially in such remote areas. One can imagine that blaming wolves for a local human atrocity might be only too convenient.

Wolves depend on large tracts of habitat and substantial populations of their principal prey species to be successful. There are three major threats to them—disease, in-breeding with dogs, and man. The decline of wolf numbers in recent times is well illustrated with the story of Wisconsin, where

Right: As humans became farmers, so they came into conflict with wolves and the cycle of predation began. It is hard to think of this protected animal as a man-eating beast—but that's what the stories from childhood, such as Little Red Riding Hood, would have us believe.

Wolves

300 years ago there were about 20,000 wolves. In 1957 there were none, although currently this has risen to about 100 in the north.

The fall in wolf numbers began when white settlers arrived in the 1830s. They started to clear the land to build farms, roads, and towns, and also hunted to extinction the elk and bison which the wolves relied on for survival. Most of these settlers were of direct European descent, where wolves were always the bad guys of legend and folklore. Life was hard enough as it was, and any threats to this, real or imagined, were met with little sympathy. Consequently, any wolves in the vicinity were wiped out. In Wisconsin this led to bounty money being paid in 1865. The laws were changed in 1957, but by then wolves were long gone.

The story is very similar worldwide, although the wolf has not been brought as close to extinction as many other animals. Some wolves have gone extinct—we have already discussed the North American dire wolf; the Falkland Island wolf was exterminated at the end of the last century, and seven sub-species have also gone extinct in the last 75 years, including the Newfoundland white wolf, *Canis lupus beothucus*, the last of which died in 1911. In Japan the Shamanu, *Canis lupus hodophilax*, was hunted to extinction in 1905. It was small for a wolf—just 14in (35.6cm) at the shoulder, smaller than many dogs.

Despite this, there are currently about 100,000 wolves in the wild—the vast majority of which are gray wolves—roughly 60,000 in Canada, 30,000 in Russia, 5,000 in Europe, 400 in China, and 10,000 in the USA. By far the most wolves in the USA are in Alaska, with about 7,000, followed by Minnesota with about 2,000.

Above and Right: It's when you see them hunt and kill that you realize the fairy stories are based on truth. They are excellent pack hunters.

18

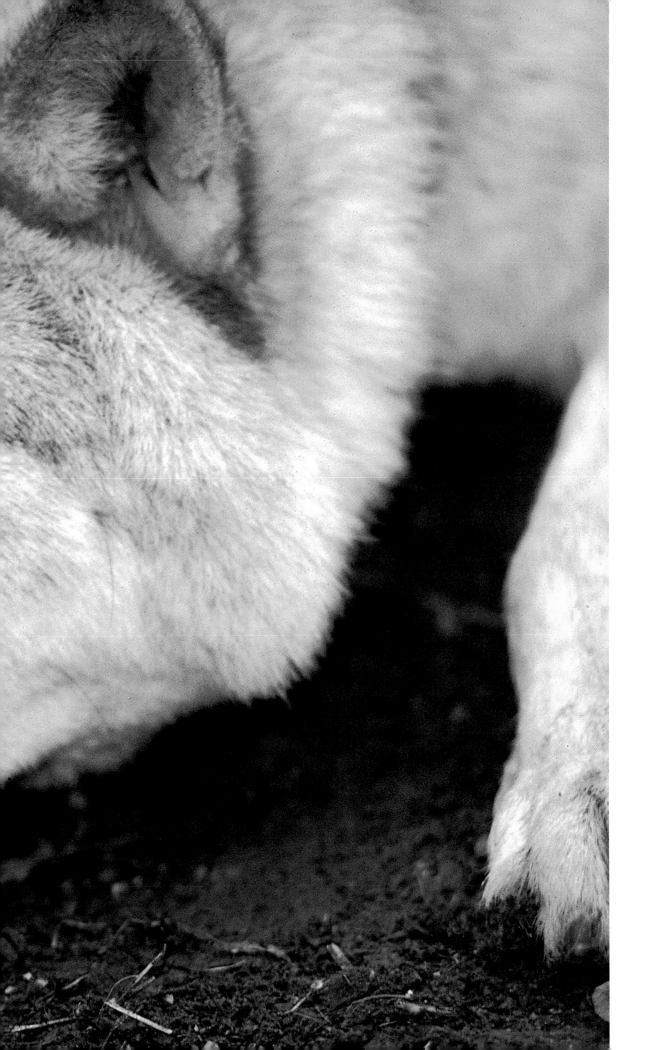

WOLF TYPES

The Gray Wolf

Previous Page and Left: This wolf is showing the classic "threat" expression.

Right: This is dominance in action — the upper wolf is imposing dominance on the other. Notice the relative ear positions of these two.

Next page: Wolves can vary greatly in color. This individual is demonstrating the lighter end of the spectrum.

The gray wolf is known by many names, including the timber wolf, the tundra wolf, the Arctic wolf, the buffalo wolf, the lobo wolf, and so on. Many of these names refer to specific sub-species, such as *Canis lupus tundrarium*, which is the Alaskan tundra wolf, or the Mexican wolf, *Canis lupus baileyi*. Whatever "common" name is used, the wolf goes under the Latin, or scientific name, of *Canis lupus*. It is the primeval member of the dog family, which makes it the ancestral origin of all domesticated dogs.

Of all the wild canids, the gray wolf is the largest, but the largest individuals are, however, in the most northerly parts of their range. A large male can stand 30in (76cm) at the shoulder and weigh 175lb (nearly 80kg), although this size is exceptional. They are also variable in color, tending to be similar to that of their habitat. Typically they will live for anywhere between 8 and 16 years, although they have lived for over 20 in captivity.

The variations in the gray wolf's territory size can be enormous, ranging from 20sq miles to 5,000 (52 to 13,000sq km)! Only mankind has a larger natural range than this. Wolf packs normally vary in size between two and twelve individuals, although there have been reports of packs as large as 40. They will be dominated by the strongest male, who will choose the strongest female as his mate—they are then known as the "alpha" pair. The younger members will constantly try to improve their standing within the dominance hierarchy—as soon as a superior wolf shows signs of weakness through age or ill-health, the younger ones will try to assert themselves.

Wolves

Wolves

The alpha pair are the only ones likely to breed, and will usually try to prevent other pack members from mating through aggressive behavior. This is to ensure that their offspring have the maximum chance of survival. One of the consequences of humans killing wolves is that the pack often splits up. This removes the mating restrictions imposed by the alpha pair, which can result in many pack members raising pups. This can produce a massive rise in wolf numbers over a comparatively short period of time.

The time of year when gray wolves mate varies from January at low altitudes, to April at higher altitudes. Their courtship may last anywhere from a few days to several months, depending on their circumstances. Oestrus itself may last from five to fifteen days, and the gestation period lasts about 63 days. The usual litter is composed of anywhere between two and eleven pups.

The young pups are born in a den, which is often a hole commandeered from other animals, or sometimes a small cave. Whenever possible, these dens are situated near water, for the obvious reason of having a drinking supply. Sometimes they have an entrance tunnel up to twenty feet long, which then opens onto a chamber. No bedding material is used in the dens, which are only used for rearing young.

The pups are blind and deaf when born, and weigh about a pound (450g). They are completely dependent on their mothers for around two months, with their eyes opening at about two weeks. By the age of three weeks, they start exploring the big bad world outside, and are normally weaned by the

Right: This young pup is checking that it's safe to come out of the den and play.

Below right: The pup stays close to the mouth of the den, and no doubt there's an adult keeping a wary eye out for predators, or youthful misbehavior! This is how a healthy pup should look—notice the clear eyes and good coat condition.

Below: Wolves can run for long distances at a relaxed pace. They do this mostly to wear down their prey—those that can't keep ahead are generally the old, the weak, or the very young.

Wolves

age of six to eight weeks. They are assisted in this by other members of the pack who act as "uncles" and "aunts;" these regurgitate partially digested food to the pups as a reflex to their begging. When times are hard, some or all of the pups may die of malnutrition, and if they are really bad, reproduction may cease altogether.

Young wolves reach sexual maturity by the time they are one-year-old, and may well leave the pack at two. When they do so, they often become solitary for a while, during which time they will seek a mate, and then pair up. The mortality rate of wolves is highest during this solitary period, mostly because they are young and inexperienced, and are covering large areas full of hazards whilst wandering. Once paired, they will form their own territory and raise their own young.

When things are normal, they are active during both the day and night, but during very cold weather, they are more active in daylight hours. In the summer the pack usually sets out to hunt in the early evening, returning to the den by the next morning. If, however, they aren't using a den, such as during the winter, they don't frequent any particular location.

When the pack is traveling, it tends to do so in single file—this makes progress through snow much easier as the first individual creates a furrow through which the others walk. When hunting they often travel along the edges of lakes and rivers as this is where prey tends to congregate. They often cover 20 miles (32km) in a day at a trot of 5-7mph (8-11kph), although they can reach 50mph (80kph) when running flat out!

Their normal method of hunting involves chasing prey for long periods at around 10-15mph (16-24kph); this separates out the weaker members of the herd. When hunting like this nearly all the adults and yearlings take part, because it requires several wolves to bring down an animal the size of a caribou or a moose. The only individuals that don't take part are those guarding any pups.

Above Left and Above: This individual shows that wolves can be very dark indeed. Compare this coat color to that of the wolf on pages 23 and 24.

Right: Wolves have a very large footprint to help them deal with soft snow—this allows them to pursue and catch prey in conditions such as those shown here.

Left: Time for a rest! The pup's coat matches in well with the local soil, providing extra concealment from predators, and in the future, from prey.

Above: Pups play in the grass. The one in the foreground is stalking something—a leaf maybe? Or is it something more substantial like a fly? Wolves start to learn their hunting skills at this tender age, gradually moving up to real prey.

Right: Having worn each other out with their strenuous play, it's time for a communal rest session. Even at this early age, they show definite signs of hierarchical behavior, with some individuals clearly displaying dominance.

Next Page: It's not just the cubs that like to rest: here two wolves sun themselves on a suitable rock ledge.

There are many sub-species of the gray wolf, most of which are listed below. Some of these are now extinct, and some are the subject of argument as to their validity.

Scientific name	Common name	Location/Remarks
Canis lupus lupus	European gray wolf, Common wolf	
C. l. arabs		Saudi Arabia
C. l. alces	Kennai Peninsula wolf	Alaska
C. l. albus	Tundra or Turukhan wolf	Finland, Kamchatka Peninsula
C. l. arctos	Melville Island wolf	Melville Island to Ellesmere Island
C. l. baileyi	Mexican wolf	Originally Sierra Madre, West Mexico
C. l. beothucus	Newfoundland White wolf	
C. l. bernardi	Banks Island tundra wolf	Northwest Territories
C. l. campestris	Steppe wolf	Western Russia
C. l. chanco		Tibet, Mongolia, Western China
C. l. columbianus	British Columbian wolf	British Columbia, Canada
C. l. crassodon	Vancouver Island wolf	
C. l. cubanensis	Causcasian wolf	Same animal as Steppe wolf
C. l. deitanus		European grey wolf sub-species reported from Spain
C. l. desertorum		Same animal as Steppe wolf
C. l. dybowski	Kamchatka wolf	May not be a valid sub-species, may be *C. l. albus*
C. l. fuscus	Cascade Mountain wolf	SW British Columbia, Canada
C. l. griseoalbus		Central Manitoba and N. Saskatchewan
C. l. hodophilax	Japanese Shamanu wolf	
C. l. hudsonicus	Hudson Bay wolf	North West Hudson Bay

Above left: This is the low-profile, nose to the ground, tracking stance . . .

Left: . . . contrasting well with this "standing tall" posture.

Right: A relaxed and healthy Eurasian wolf—the coat is in good condition, the eyes are clear, and the posture shows confidence.

Wolves

Left and Right: Facial markings are prominent personal characteristics of wolves and—as with dogs—it takes only a short time before individuals can be identified.

Next Page: Another striking individual from the tundra.

Scientific name	Common name	Location/Remarks
C. l. irremotus	Northern Rocky Mountain wolf	
C. l. italicus		European grey wolf sub-species reported from Italy
C. l. labradorius	Labrador wolf	N. Quebec and Labrador
C. l. laniger	Tibetan wolf	China, Mongolia, Tibet, SW. Russia
C. l. ligoni	Alexander Archipelago wolf	SE Alaska inc. Alexander Arch.
C. l. lycaon	Eastern or Timber wolf	Ontario, Quebec, Northern Minnesota
C. l. mackenzii	Mackenzie tundra wolf	Mackenzie River to Gt. Bear Lake
C. l. manningi	Baffin Island wolf	Baffin Island and others nearby
C. l. mogollonensis	Mogollon Mountain wolf	Central Arizona and New Mexico
C. l. monstrabilis	Texas Gray wolf	Western Texas and NE Mexico
C. l. nubilus	Great Plains, Prairie, Buffalo wolf	Great Plains
C. l. occidentalis	Mackenzie Valley wolf	Mackenzie River to Central Alberta
C. l. orion	Greenland wolf	Greenland
C. l. pallipes		India to Iraq
C. l. pambasileus	Interior Alaskan wolf	Alaskan interior
C. l. signatus		European gray wolf sub-species reported from Spain
C. l. tundarum	Alaskan Tundra wolf	Alaskan Arctic coast
C. l. variabilis		Near East (extinct)
C. l. youngi	Southern Rocky Mountain wolf	Nevada, Utah, Colorado

Wolves

The Red Wolf

Left: This picture shows why red wolves were mistaken for coyote/ wolf hybrids for years. They look much more jackal-like than gray wolves.

Right: The face of a red wolf is thinner than that of a gray.

The red wolf (*Canis rufus*) is considered by some to be a hybrid of gray wolves and coyotes, and therefore not a true wolf. As this is a question of taxonomic classification, we will leave this debate to the biologists.

The red wolf is a shy, secretive animal that preys mostly on a variety of small to medium sized mammals, from rodents to white-tailed deer. It is not as pack-oriented as the gray wolf, and it's believed they mate for life.

At present the red wolf has a "endangered" status under the Federal Endangered Species Act, although there are those who would have it removed from the list if they could. It was considered extinct in the wild by 1980, although it once roamed throughout the south-eastern United States.

In the 1970s a captive breeding program was started by trapping the last 14 red wolves in the wild. These were then placed in captive breeding facilities. That the program was successful was demonstrated by the release into the wild of 71 captive-bred animals between 1987 and 1997. The Alligator River and Pocosin Lakes National Wildlife Refuges were chosen as the release sites. There have also been 37 more released into the Great Smoky Mountains National Park. Today there are about 275 red wolves at 40 different locations, including about 80 in the wild.

Red Wolf Subspecies

Scientific name	Common name	Location/Remarks	Extinct
C. rufus rufus	Texas red wolf	Texas	
C. rufus gregoryi	Mississippi Valley red wolf		
C. rufus floridanus	Florida red wolf		

Left: Notice, when viewed from the front, how big the red wolf's ears are in comparison with those of a gray.

Right: Two photographs of red wolves released from captivity and returned to a more natural domain. Before their return to the wild, they were fitted with radio collars. This was partly to placate the local human populace, and partly to allow scientists to monitor their movements.

Wolves

Red wolves are more solitary than gray wolves, mainly because they tend to hunt much smaller prey. The presence of several wolves would be difficult when hunting animals such as ground squirrels.

Wolves

Left and Right: Once again, note that facial markings allow clear distinction between individuals.

Below: The radio collar can be seen clearly on this red wolf.

Next Page: The more angular features of the red wolf are obvious in this photograph.

The Ethiopian Wolf

The Ethiopian wolf (*Canis simensis*) is probably the most endangered large mammal in the world. Until recently many considered it to be a jackal, but modern DNA techniques have shown that it is in fact a true wolf, which makes it the only one in Africa. It has also been known over the years as the Abyssinian wolf, the Simien jackal, the Ethiopian jackal, and the Simien fox.

Whatever you call it, the Ethiopian wolf is a rare and mysterious animal, about which little is known. It's smaller than the gray wolf, standing at only about 23in (58cm) at the shoulder, with the larger individuals weighing about 39lb (17.7kg).

They are restricted entirely to the mountains of Ethiopia, usually between 10,000 and 16,500ft (3,050-5,030m) above sea level. They are one of the most endangered canids in the world, surviving mostly off small animals such as the mole rat and other rodents. There is evidence that they are also opportunists, scavenging when they are able to. They are very social, although they seem to hunt singly. This would fit in with a diet of rodents—there's not much to be gained from hunting mice in packs!

The mating season lasts from autumn through to winter, with birth taking place about nine weeks after conception. There may be up to seven pups in the litter, in a den usually located amongst rocks. There is communal rearing of the young, with often up to seven yearlings and adults taking part.

One of the greatest pressures on their numbers is that their pelts are held in high esteem locally. This has resulted in the remaining Ethiopian wolves becoming nocturnal, making it even harder to gauge their present population. The political situation in Ethiopia meant that in recent years it was impossible to survey them, but recent counts are depressing. In 1976 there were a possible 700 in the Bale Mountains National Park, but this has dropped now to only around 150. It's thought that there are fewer than 500 left in total.

They are protected by law in Ethiopia, and most of those surviving are in national parks, but it's difficult to know how effective the enforcement is. One of the greatest threats to their survival continues to be domestic dogs, partly by interbreeding, and partly by the introduction of canid diseases. Another threat is the ever-present problem of over-grazing of their territory by domestic cattle, sheep, and goats. Finally, as if all these threats were not enough, the Ethiopian wolf is remarkably tame, making it easy prey for hunters.

The Maned Wolf

The maned wolf, *Chrysocyon brachyurus*, is not a true wolf in strict taxonomic terms. It looks like a cross between a jackal and a long-legged wolf. It is, however, actually closer to foxes than either. It is a reddish color, with a pale belly and large fox-like ears. Maned wolves have long, soft fur, which is thicker around the neck, giving them the look of a mane, from whence their name is derived. This fur is of little commercial value, but is regulated by inclusion in Appendix II of CITES, the Convention on International Trade in Endangered Species of Wild Fauna and Flora.

As with many endangered species having to survive the encroachments of mankind, the maned wolf has a much reduced range, with as few as 2,200 left alive. They are found in South America, chiefly in Brazil and Northern Argentina, but also in Paraguay, Uruguay, and Bolivia, although in the last two their population is very low, and may even be non-existent. They are protected by law in Argentina and Bolivia. Fossil evidence from the mid-Pleistocene onwards suggests the they have never existed anywhere but the South American continent.

Their habitat is typically savannah and swampland, which is one reason why they have evolved long legs—so they can see over the top of the long grass and reeds. In spite of having these long legs, the maned wolf is not a particularly fast runner. An adult can be up to 29in (74cm) at the shoulder, and weigh an average of 44lb (20kg).

They are opportunistic in their feeding habits, with an omnivorous palette. They will eat everything from small mammals through to birds, insects, and fruit. Unfortunately, they are often shot or trapped by local farmers who are understandably fed up with having their chickens eaten by hungry wolves.

Maned wolves are normally solitary, except in the breeding season. Mating may take place anywhere from December through to June, and the pups will be born about 65 days later. The normal litter is of two to four pups, born in a den, often above ground. The rearing is undertaken by both parents, who will regurgitate food for their young for up to ten months.

One of the problems with trying to conserve this species is that they do very badly in captivity, partly due to a disease called cystinuria, for which vets have yet to find a cure. The young generally don't breed until they are two years old, and even when they do breed in captivity, the pups have a very high mortality rate.

At the time of writing, there are about 85 maned wolves in various zoos around the world in a project called the "Species Survival Plan." The idea is to re-introduce them when there is enough natural habitat conserved for them to survive in.

Next page: Gray wolves are more numerous and less endangered than such rarities as the Ethiopian wolf.

The Arctic "Wolf"

This common name is given to two very different animals. Some people use it to refer to the Arctic populations of gray wolf, and others to the Arctic fox. This latter, as its name would suggest, is an animal of the tundra and Arctic, although there is also a population in the Altai mountains in Central Asia. The scientific name is *Alopex lagopus*.

Above: Often called the "Arctic Wolf," the Arctic fox is considerably smaller than the gray wolf.

The Prairie Wolf

Right: You can see why a coyote could be mistaken for a wolf at a distance, especially to someone not familiar with the real thing! Coyotes have benefited by the demise of the wolf, taking over most of its former ranges. They hunt small animals, or scavenge wherever the opportunity presents itself. They have made themselves particularly unpopular with farmers, who waste little time in killing them, and hanging their corpses out for all to see, often on roadside fences.

Below right: Coyotes howl too, but not as convincingly as the real thing!

This is another name for the coyote, *Canis latrans*. One of the greatest explorer-artists of all time, pioneer-explorer John James Audubon, used the name in his outstanding book on American mammals.

Extinct Wolves

Left and Next Page: Man has already made a number of wolf species extinct: unless we are careful, the whole family will go that way.

The Dire Wolf

At the height of its tenure, the dire wolf's range covered most of the western hemisphere. It has been extinct for a long time now: the last ones finally died out about 8,000 to 9,000 years ago. American myth and legend would have us believe that it was a menacing creature with piercing eyes and massive fangs. In reality, however, it was very similar to the contemporary gray wolf, but of a heavier build. It was a large animal, growing to 6ft 6in (two meters) in length, and due to its heavy dentition, it is thought to have had its jaws primarily adapted to crush bones. It was at one time the most common predator in North America.

The first discovery of the dire wolf was by Francis A. Linck in the summer of 1854; he found a fossilized jawbone in the bed of the Ohio River. He refused to let the scientists see it, but after he died the jawbone was passed on to a Dr. Leidy in Philadelphia. He identified it as a new species, and the scientific name of *Canis dirus Leidy* was made official in 1858.

The bulk of the knowledge gained about the dire wolf has come from the tar pits at Rancho La Brea, in the heart of Los Angeles. These tar pits are naturally occurring black ponds of sticky liquid formed by oil rising to the surface. As this is the only place in the world that this happens, it is perhaps not surprising that animals did not realize that they were in danger. This resulted in lots of them falling in, which then attracted the attention of carrion eaters, who also fell in. As a consequence, it is one of the world's richest Ice Age fossil sites, providing us with a unique record of the plant and animal life which existed between 10,000 and 40,000 years ago.

With the passage of time, each pit would get filled in by wind-blown leaves and other detritus, and would disappear. The oil would then rise elsewhere forming a new pit. Over the years, many have come and gone, each of them leaving a massive fossil record. Only a few pits have been fully excavated, but even so there have been over 3,600 skeletons of the dire wolf recovered, more than any other species of mammal. The range of skeletons recovered is amazing, from humming birds to mammoths. If you're ever in the vicinity, go and visit the tar pits—the display of wolf skeletons alone is well worth the time!

Some believe that the physiology of the dire wolf indicates that it was primarily a carrion eater, while others suggest that the large numbers found in the tar pits indicate that they hunted in large packs. Evidence from the fossil record at Rancho La Brea demonstrates that they were often injured in a manner similar to that of gray wolves when hunting large prey like moose. These tended to be "kick" wounds to the head and ribs, sometimes fatal, but more often the individuals recovered. Other animals capable of delivering these injuries included the wild horse, the bison, the mastodon, and mammoths.

This is testament to the dire wolf living in packs similar to the gray wolf. Quite simply, an injured wolf would have starved to death without the assistance of its pack members.

The Marsupial Wolf

In Australia until recent times there was an animal variously called the Marsupial wolf, the Tasmanian wolf, the Tasmanian tiger, or the thylacine. At one time it was also found on Papua New Guinea, as well as on mainland Australia, and the island of Tasmania. In reality though, it was not a wolf.

The scientific name is *Thylacinus cynocephalus*, which means "pouched dog with a wolf head." The head was very dog-like, but perhaps the most remarkable thing about it was the gape—they could open their powerful jaws until they were nearly in a straight line. This, coupled with their very long incisors, meant they were formidable predators. Their prey consisted of kangaroos, wallabies, and various small mammals and birds, which they killed by crushing the skull.

Like other marsupials, the female carried its young in a pouch, which opened backwards. It was recorded as mating between September and October, and bearing three to four young in November or December. A fully grown thylacine stood about two feet (61cm) at the shoulder, and was about six feet (1.83m) long, including the tail. The most obviously distinguishing feature was the series of banded stripes along the flanks, which gave rise to the name "Tasmanian tiger." Their tracks could be easily separated from those of a dog or true wolf because they had five toes, unlike the four of a canid.

It is thought that the thylacine was made extinct on the Australian mainland by the arrival of the Dingo, which never spread to Tasmania, around 1000 BC. When white settlers arrived, it was common there, although once sheep farming began, the thylacine was soon reduced dramatically in numbers. This was encouraged when in 1888 the Tasmanian government placed a bounty on thylacines. Whilst their skins were also in great demand, some believe that the final collapse in the thylacine population was due to a disease spread by white settlers.

There were attempts to keep thylacines in captivity, such as by the Royal Zoological Society of Australia, which opened the Adelaide Zoological Gardens to the public on April 25, 1883. Their records show that they had

Wolves

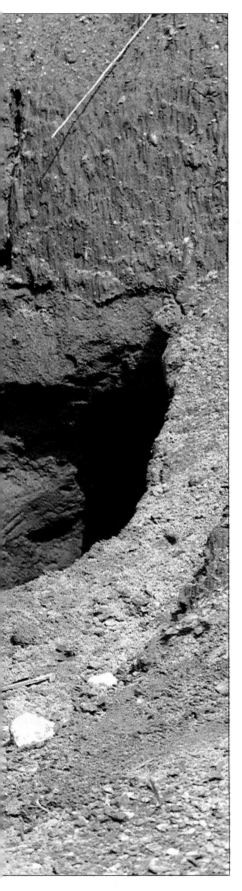

two in their collection in 1886, which they acquired from Tasmania, and they added to this with two more in 1889. The list, however, only details two in the collection in 1891. It is not known whether two died, or were moved to another zoo. Another pair was obtained in 1897, and yet another pair in 1898, but by 1904, the animal was no longer listed. It is perhaps indicative of how little importance the zoo attached to the thylacine in that almost no records were kept regarding where they were obtained, their condition on arrival, or their health or habits throughout their stay.

Although no zoos managed to breed them in captivity, they generally lived for more than eight years. It is not known how this related to the animal in the wild. Unfortunately the last one died in Hobart Zoo in 1934. It is generally believed that the last wild thylacine was hunted down and killed in 1930, although the Tasmanian government declared it a protected species in 1938. While most authorities on the subject believe the thylacine to be extinct, there have been many unproved recordings. One of these was in Northern Victoria in 1977 when there was a possible sighting of a group of eight, including a mother with pups.

If you're wondering whether it's possible that the thylacine still exists somewhere, it has to be remembered that it was by nature a shy and retiring animal, which lived in remote areas. This alone would make it hard enough to find, but it was also nocturnal, which would make the task even more daunting. Australia is a big place, so let's hope that one day they are found thriving in some far-flung corner!

The Falkland Island Wolf

While this species was not a true wolf, it was also known as the Antarctic wolf. Its scientific name is *Dusicyon australis*. It used to live on the West and East Falkland Islands, which are in the South Atlantic, off the coast of Argentina. The local people called it the "warrah." The government sealed its fate when it placed a bounty on its head in 1839. The fashion trade caught on to its thick fur, and large numbers of pelts were sent to New York to satisfy demand. Not surprisingly, it could not survive the impact on its numbers from hunting, poisoning, and trapping. It finally became extinct when the last one was killed at Shallow Bay in 1876.

It stood about 24 inches (61cm) tall at the shoulder, and generally resembled the gray wolf, although its legs were shorter. No one knows how it reached the Falklands, which are a long way offshore. It is possible that its ancestors crossed on an ice-shelf in the last Ice Age, during the Pleistocene. Another idea is that they were introduced by early settlers. This last suggestion might explain why they were exceptionally tame, even whilst being hunted to extinction.

It is thought that the Falkland Island wolf originally ate penguins and other small animals before domestic stock arrived with the white settlers. The first description of this species came from a British sailor serving on HMS *Welfare* which visited around 1689. They were later massacred by Spanish settlers who would lure them with a piece of meat held in one hand, then stabbing them with a knife held in the other. They were also poisoned in large numbers by sheep farmers. London Zoo managed to get one individual in 1868, but sadly this was before they started acquiring enough animals to start a breeding program.

BEHAVIOR

Wolves

Pack and Social Life

The social life of the wolf was seen for years as one of dominance through strength—the "law of the jungle." More recently, scientists such as David L. Mech have been saying that this is all wrong, and that the "old beliefs" were based on unnatural behavior as a result of captivity. It now appears that in the wild, the wolf is in fact much more familial, and much less aggressive than previously thought. That is, of course, unless you're on the menu!

Their social structure is very complicated—basically there are two separate hierarchies, one for the males and one for the females. The most senior animal in each of these is called the "alpha" individual. When it comes to the mating season, only the alpha male will mate, and usually only with the alpha female, although there are several documented cases when secondary females mated with the alpha male as well.

The only time that the alpha pair cannot prevent others mating is when they are coupled—they cannot separate for about 30 minutes. During this time it is possible for others to attempt to mate, but normally the rest of the pack will drive them apart. During the rest of the year, the wolves are generally very friendly towards each other, with a large amount of face-licking and other pack-bonding behavior.

The alpha female bears a litter of up to ten pups in May or June, in a remote den. The whole pack usually assists in the upbringing by feeding the mother and pups with prey from their hunting. They will also look after the pups while the mother goes hunting herself. Some of the females will act as

Wolves

surrogate mothers by undergoing "phantom pregnancies," which means they produce milk, but no pups. They will also guard the area against predators like grizzly bears. When the pups are old enough, the pack once again becomes more nomadic. This is usually around the fall.

The size of a wolf pack is closely linked to its predominant prey. If the territory contains abundant large animals like moose and caribou, the pack size will also be large so that they can hunt in large numbers. They will also defend their territory against other wolves. If the main prey is migratory, such as caribou, the wolf pack will often follow them for long distances. Wolves are thoroughly opportunistic, and will prey on anything from caribou to mice, and even spawning salmon.

Wolf dens are often used by many succeeding generations, but the truth is that no one knows for how long good sites may be used: it could be for many hundreds or even thousands of years. Another mystery is just how wolves survive through the long, dark winters of the Arctic north. The pups are only about a third grown when winter starts, and fully grown come the end, even though temperatures may be -122°F (-50°C). That some do not survive is a certainty, but what the successful ones feed on is not yet fully understood.

Below: Wolves are opportunistic—they will range widely looking out for an easy meal.

Above Right: Here's a full-on howling session in progress. Each wolf will hold a different note, possibly thereby communicating how many individuals there are—a wider spread of tones would indicate a bigger pack.

Below Right: The ritualized gestures and postures of pack life are always important, whether at play or in earnest.

Left: The pack co-operates in making a kill, and then all get to eat some of it. Those lower down in the hierarchy may have to wait, such as the individual on the left. Notice the ear position, and general body posture—positive signs of submission.

Below Left: Much of a pack's social life is centered around the den, with raising pups being the major focus of the year. Dens are often situated amongst rocks or, as here, located between tree roots. This helps to keep out uninvited guests, such as hungry bears.

Right: Pack life can involve all sorts of tussles and competitions. This is a play fight over a piece of mule-deer hide.

Wolves

Left: There's no getting away from it: wolves are remarkably photogenic!

Below Left: Notice that, when sniffing the ground, wolves still keep their ears up, alert for the slightest sound.

Right: This picture shows well how wolves keep their feet in a line when walking. This allows them to make headway through snow much more easily than if they had to plow their way through with all four feet.

Left: You can see here how the legs
are used when jumping. This is
quite different from their synchro-
nization when running or walking.

Wolves

Above: Compare the leg movement in this photograph with that on pages 70 and 71. The timing of the leg movements changes as speed increases or decreases.

Left: Wolves tend to travel in single file, partly for the same reason as mentioned before—it's much more economical to only make one path when travelling through thick snow.

Right: Close-up showing the thick coat and ruff around the neck.

Two different facial expressions—

Above: You don't want to mess with me.

Left: You REALLY don't want to mess with me!

Wolves

Wolves

Previous Pages: Lone gray wolf on the Alaskan tundra.

Left: A wolf's ears are wonderfully expressive—this one has spotted something . . .

Below Left: . . . while this one is creeping up on something.

Right: Seeing a wolf in the wild is quite an achievement; at best a glimpse through the trees is all you can hope for—and that's at a zoo!

Next Pages: Spot the difference! Coyote on left; gray wolf on right.

Howling and Communication

The gray wolf has a variety of communication methods—visual, olfactory, and auditory. They can make sounds from low growls through to barks and, of course, they howl. Humans can hear howls up to ten miles away, although wolves rarely respond to howls further than seven miles away.

There are many reasons why wolves howl, from calling the pack together, to signalling their presence to others. Sometimes a howling session signals the start of a hunt; at others it designates the start of scent marking. This is done by regularly scratching and depositing urine and faeces at certain points around the boundary of the pack's territory. It is done not only to warn other wolves whose territory it is, but also to signal reproductive condition, which helps establish new packs.

A communal howling session starts with one wolf, the others usually joining in within a few howls. Each wolf produces a series of single howls, which last up to eleven seconds each. When wolves are on their own, they typically howl for a total of around 35 seconds, but when they are in a pack, the howling is longer.

One of the people to have studied wolf howls first hand is Lois Crisler, who observed her own tame wolves as well as those in the wild. She noted that, when a wolf is howling, it will do so on a note that is distinct from any others being produced. If she joined in with a howl of her own that was on the same note as one being made by a wolf, it would shift its howl to a different note.

Wolves

Above and Right: This mule-deer buck is providing a good meal for these two gray wolves, one of which is a black color-phase individual.

Left: Facial interaction is fundamental to wolf communication, with the black animal showing overt submission to the other.

Wolves

Wolves also make several other sounds, one of which is the whimper or whine. This is hard to study in the wild, as the sound is too quiet for all but close observers. The whimper is a sound of intimacy—one of greeting or submission. The opposite is true of growling, which is the sound of threat or aggression. All those of us who have ever had contact with domestic dogs will be familiar with both of these sounds, but the one with which we will be most familiar is barking. A bark is produced either in alarm, or as a threat to intruders.

Wolves make many visual signals to each other, including tail posture, ear position, facial expression, and body attitude. Facial expressions are used between wolves when they are close to each other. They can be in the form of "smiles," which usually indicate friendly greetings, but they can also be in the form of snarls with the lips curled back exposing the teeth. Not surprisingly, snarls indicate aggression, and are usually accompanied by growls. When a wolf is signalling aggression, it will also raise its hackles to make itself look bigger; it will have its ears up, and its tail either horizontal, or raised.

When an individual greets a dominant wolf, it will gesture submission with one of several postures, such as roll-over, which is the most extreme form. For a less severe gesture it may hold its head down, and keep its tail low, often crouching at the same time. When the intention is a friendly greeting, it may "bounce" from side to side, which is a form of play gesture. Other friendly gestures include the well-known tail wag, accompanied by the "smile" expression mentioned earlier.

Below: Wolves can signal to each other in many ways, including body postures, scent, and sound . . .

Right: . . . as this wolf demonstrates.

# Wolves

Left: While this is a beautiful photo of a wolf howling at the moon—the image itself, and the images it evokes, are inexact. To begin with wolves will, in fact, howl at any time of day or night, and the involvement of the moon says more about the imagination of man when listening to the eerie, ethereal howls than anything else.

Wolves

Above: The fact that these two gray wolves are playing is not stopping the one on the right displaying dominance over the other.

Left and Right: Two more views of individuals howling.

Wolves

Left: The lower dentition is easily examined here—those canines look capable of some serious damage!

Below: A howl doesn't need to be too strenuous—why waste energy standing, when you can howl lying down?

Right: There's always something interesting to sniff when you're a wolf! Scent is—as with all the canids—an important method of communication.

Next pages: Two close-ups of gray wolves.

Wolves

Wolves

Above: Canids in general are excellent runners, able to sustain high speeds for considerable lengths of time. Wolves—as western fiction has done its best to confirm—can cover substantial ranges with their "lope."

Left: This wolf is about to start howling—it has raised its muzzle, but has not yet closed its eyes, and opened its mouth.

Right: The size of a wolf's feet can be seen clearly here—compare them to those of a domestic dog, and you'll see the difference.

Wolves

Wolves

Above: The different color phases are well exemplified in this pack.

Left: It may look black, but it's a gray wolf and that mule deer is good!

Right: Splendid wintertime portrait of the gray wolf.

THE WOLF TODAY

Reintroduction and Conservation Schemes

Left: This wolf has just spotted dinner—it remains to be seen whether dinner has spotted the wolf!

Right: This wolf wouldn't look so relaxed if it knew that ranchers were so influential with federal judges able to order the cessation of reintroduction schemes.

As indicated earlier, there are about 100,000 wild wolves worldwide, and many countries are looking at wolf reintroduction and conservation schemes. One of the most publicized reintroduction schemes is that at the Yellowstone National Park, where 14 gray wolves were released to form what was hoped would be a breeding colony. So far there have been an unfortunate number of deaths, many of which have been due to illegal shooting. At least one of these was shot by a ranch worker on March 30, 1996; he was subsequently fined $500, not much for the life of an endangered animal. All hope is not lost, however, as the wolves are breeding successfully, and the current population stands at about 80.

Nothing is ever simple when it comes to conserving wolves, however, for some of the ranchers around Yellowstone petitioned a federal judge, who then ruled that the reintroduction program was illegal, and that the wolves must be removed. At the time of writing, the removal order has been "stayed," pending an appeal by the conservationists. It is ironic that the argument made by the ranchers was that introduced wolves could harm naturally migrating wolves from Canada and Montana, as though that would worry them!

Generally the Yellowstone wolves are doing very well because of the large number of prey animals in the reserve. The yearling pups are also growing very large: one of them weighed 120lb (54.5kg)! One of the biggest

Wolves

adults was an individual known as "28M," who weighed 140lb (63.5kg) when he was illegally shot in the winter of 1997.

The governor of the state of Alaska is considering a report he commissioned by the US National Academy of Sciences Research Council. If he follows its recommendations, it should halt the wholesale slaughter of wolves. One of the problems is that those trying to conserve the wolf have to fight the vested interests of the Alaskan Board of Game and the Department of Fish and Game. They want to boost the numbers of caribou and moose so that hunters can pay to shoot them. To do this they want to wipe out all predatory species, including, of course, the wolf.

In the past, the US State Veterinary Service deliberately infected wolves with sarcoptic mange—a debilitating parasitic skin disease—to control their numbers. Another of the particularly nasty ways of achieving control is by "saturation snaring." Fortunately for the future of wolves, although too late for many, harrowing television pictures of dead and dying wolves forced the governor to suspend these measures pending the results of a scientific study. He has stated that control must be based on good economic principles, something that the studies do not uphold.

The frontier mentality of killing all predators to safeguard livestock is going out of fashion, and public support is outnumbering the farm lobby where it counts—in the voting booth. This is where modern conservation can be most effective, as there is one thing that a politician will be certain to

Above: Playtime! This is the classical play posture—body crouched, front legs splayed, and a challenging "well come on then!" expression.

Right: Wolves are making a comeback in many places, such as in the south of France, in the Massif du Mercantour.

act on, and that is anything that will win him guaranteed votes. The importance of the tourist dollar to places like Alaska can make a real difference to political decisions about matters like wolf conservation.

Whilst wolves are under threat in many places, in others they are making a comeback. Sometimes this is as a result of natural events, but these days this is uncommon; it is much more usual for mankind to have intervened in some manner. In France the gray wolf is slowly repopulating some of the mountainous areas, especially in the Massif du Mercantour. They disappeared from France and Germany in the 1930s, but they survived well in Scandinavia, with others hanging on in Spain, Italy, Greece, and Eastern Europe. The wolves in Italy have started to expand their range since about 1977, and have spread into the central mountainous region. More recently they have reached France, where they were first seen in November 1992. They are now established in the Parc National du Mercantour.

In Italy it was estimated in a survey over several years that six percent of the prey taken by wolves was livestock. Studies there have shown that there are methods to improve the protection of livestock from wolves, and they now have a system of technical and financial assistance to help the development of alpine sheep and dairy farming.

In September 1996 wolves around the Massifs de Gordolasque and Authion, a few miles north-west of the Col de Turini, had become enough of a nuisance that a "beat" was organized to scare them away from the area.

Wolves

Four hundred sheep and goats had been killed in the previous year, 95 percent of them in this region. This beat was done without dogs, with the intent of scaring the wolves away, but not to harm or capture them. In the Mercantour the wolves have a territory of about 20,000 acres. Their diet there consists of young or elderly ungulates, such as chamois, moufflons, deer, and boar. They also take a small number of sheep and cattle. They also eat birds, insects, rabbits, hares, marmots, and many other small animals. On top of this, they eat a large amount of fruit, up to 65 percent of their total food by weight in the summer.

Finland is, however, still issuing permits to kill bears and lynxes, and allows a five-month open season on wolves in Lapland. All of these are meant to have full protection under the European Union's Habitats Directive, but there is an exception when an animal is considered to be a serious threat to people or property. In the last five years 300 lynxes, 250 bears, and 50 wolves have been legally slaughtered. Of those, only about a dozen were actually threatening livestock, causing damage, or annoying humans. The rest were killed for sport. In Lapland the reindeer hunters are intending to exterminate the wolf entirely from Northern Finland, even though wolves only take 100 to 400 reindeer a year from the total population of 300,000. If they succeed, wolves in Norway and Sweden will be cut off from any fresh genetic input.

One of the biggest threats to wolf survival is modern transportation. In Sweden and Norway in one 18-month period, five were killed, three by cars, and two by trains. Scandinavian wolves only started breeding again south of

Wolves

the Arctic Circle in 1983, after an absence of nearly a 100 years. Unfortunately there are still those who are leaving out carrion laced with strychnine to kill wolves. This has the consequence of not only poisoning endangered wolves, but also a wide variety of other wildlife including ravens and golden eagles.

Sweden gave wolves legal protection in 1966 and Norway in 1973, but even so 14 wolves had been deliberately killed between being given this protection and 1989. The local populace are for the most part supporting conservation. In fact, when a wolf was run down with a snowmobile and then stabbed to death in April 1989, in north-central Sweden, the locals raised a massive reward for information leading to the conviction of the person responsible. This young male wolf had become something of a local celebrity by playing with local dogs in the village of Langa, in Jamtland county. It even joined in on elk-hunts by running alongside the hounds. He was filmed, appeared on television, and won friends all over Sweden.

In 1988, wolves were found breeding in Greenland for only the second time this century. They were discovered by a British expedition that

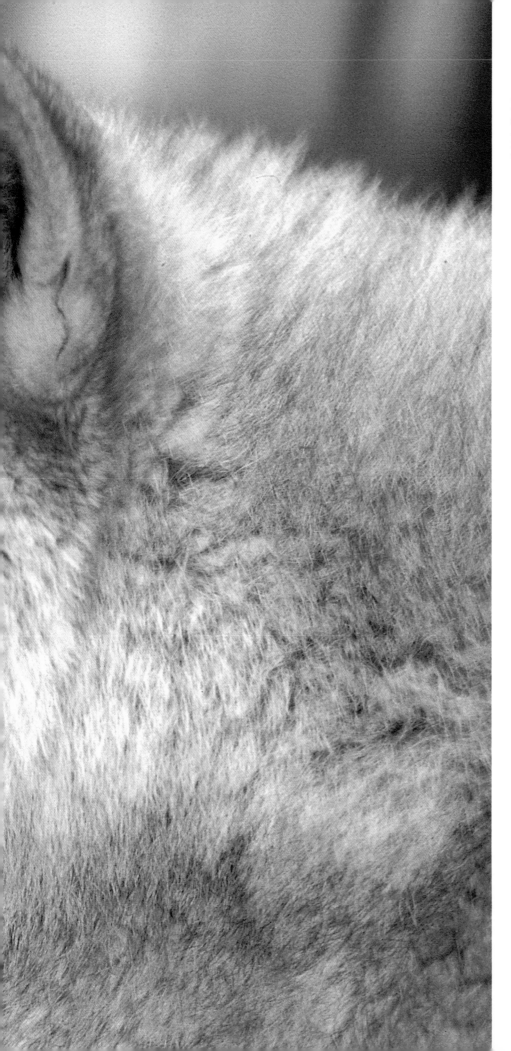

Left: Keen sight, superb hearing, and an extremely sensitive nose, provide the senses needed by a hunter.

Wolves

observed a pair of white wolves with two pups. They were exceptionally tame—the male came to within a few feet of them, and showed no aggression at all. Unfortunately this tameness resulted in the death of the female in August of that year when she approached a French "scientific" expedition—they shot her. We can do without that kind of science. A post mortem showed that she may have weaned her pups, so there is hope that they survived.

In all the countries that have resident populations of wolves, or hope to re-establish them, there are still many who are highly anti-wolf. In Norway, for instance, one of the leading campaigners for wolf protection has received death threats. In 1985, one of six wolves that were trying to establish themselves in an area on the Norwegian/Swedish border was shot by an ecstatic hunter who declared to the media that it was "the best feeling of my life." He was not defending his sheep, he did not have any—he was just a plain and simple murderer. After much publicity of the issue of wolf conservation versus extermination, a public poll found that 80% of Norwegians supported conserving their large carnivores (including wolves, lynxes, and bears).

There is hope in Norway though: for the first time in 50 years wolves have bred there, successfully raising at least six pups in two litters. The government has laid down a policy of establishing eight to ten packs, but has not provided the resources to track and study the wolves. Without this funding it will be difficult to monitor what is happening to them, and whether the hunters are still persecuting them.

Wolves

In Calgary native hunters are still massacring wolves; in the winter of 1997/8 they killed 460 before the end of February. Many are killed by hunters chasing them down with snowmobiles, and then shooting them. It is expected that this figure will rise before spring. The main reason for this slaughter is a large demand for wolf pelts.

One of the reintroduction schemes concerns the Mexican wolf, *Canis lupus baileyi*. This was first described scientifically by E. W. Nelson and E. A. Goldman from an adult male they had collected in Chihuahua, Mexico in 1899. It was named after the well-known field biologist, Vernon Bailey of the Bureau of Biological Survey. It is smaller than the gray wolf, with its weight averaging 10 pounds less, and can also be very varied in color. Formerly their range included Arizona, New Mexico, Texas, and Mexico.

The Mexican wolf, a sub-species of the gray wolf, was originally hunted down by the Government whose intent was that "no refuge for wolves was to be permitted." This was heavily influenced by wealthy cattlemen and livestock interests. On June 30, 1914, Congress declared war on wolves, and the Bureau of Biological Survey became responsible for the destruction of them and other animals considered to be a risk to livestock. They formed the Predatory Animal and Rodent Control Branch, which in its first six months killed 69 Mexican wolves and pups. Throughout the 1920s they continued to average 100 Mexican wolf kills a year, but in the 1930s this was down to only about 10 a year—presumably because they had killed most of them by that time. Due to a lack of authentication, the last wild Mexican wolf in the US was killed in either New Mexico or Texas around 1970.

A plan to save the Mexican wolf was accepted by the governments of Mexico and the United States on September 15, 1982. An inherent part of

Below: Sadly the wolf is still being massacred in places like Calgary. Reintroduction schemes are the wolf's best chance for survival in many areas.

Right: Congress' declaration of war on wolves in 1914 heralded 50 years of slaughter. Today only reintroduction will bring the wolf back into many areas of the United States.

Wolves

this plan was to establish a captive gene-pool, and from there start a reintroduction scheme. One of the problems with any breeding program is the risk of in-breeding; to combat this, many studbooks have been set up to record DNA and other genetic information. The idea is to reduce infertility and other associated problems.

As far as the reintroduction scheme was concerned, the intent was to target an area away from cattle ranching, where there would be enough deer to sustain a wolf population. This scheme has started on the Arizona/New Mexico border, in Blue Range country. One of the biggest problems is that the wolves have got to learn to fear humans, as there are many locals who would happily shoot or trap them.

Another reintroduction scheme is to help re-establish the Red wolf. On September 14, 1987, officials of the Fish and Wildlife Service released two Red wolves into the wilds of the Alligator River National Wildlife Refuge. Both of these were radio-collared. By October of the same year, three more pairs were also released into the same area. The radio collars had radio-operated darts, so that if any of the animals became a threat, they could be immobilized by remote control. It is hoped to increase the captive population to 200, and that in the wild to 30. Other suitable sites for reintroduction will also be sought. One of the encouraging things is that local hunters have taken part in this conservation work by recording sightings, and, so far, no wolves have been shot.

Above: One of the problems with reintroduction schemes is in finding a location where there are no cattle ranches, but where there are enough wild prey animals to sustain a wolf population.

Right: Reintroduction works well if there are sufficient prey animals to keep the wolves away from hen-coops and livestock.

Left: Two gray wolves in
fine condition.

Left: There is hope—some hunters are now on the wolf's side, and are assisting conservationists with recording sightings. The more this is accepted as normal by the hunting fraternity, the more chance there is for the future of the wolf.

Below left: At the outset of reintroduction programmes, there is always the risk of in-breeding. This will, however, diminish as populations join up to diversify the gene pool.

Right: Red wolf with radio collar having been reintroduced into the wild.

Wolves

Left: Red wolf at the Wild Canid Research Center, MO.

Right: Gray wolf in captivity.

Left: One day, maybe, wolves will re-populate many of their former territories, but before this happens, many old-time prejudices will have to be overcome.

Further Reading

L. David Mech, *The Wolf: the ecology and behaviour of an endangered species.* Garden City, New York: Natural History Press, 1970.

L. David Mech, *The Way of the Wolf.* Voyageur Press, 1991.

L. David Mech. *The Arctic Wolf: Ten Years With The Pack.* Stillwater, Minn. USA. 1997.

Candace Savage, *The World of the wolf.* San Francisco: Sierra Club Books. 1996.

Michael W. Fox, *Behaviour of Wolves, Dogs & Related Canids.* Krieger, Florida. 1984.

Adolph Murie, *The Wolves of Mount McKinley.* Washington DC: US Govt. Printing Office. 1944.

Durward L. Allen, *The Wolves of Minong: Their role in a wild community.* Boston, Houghton Mifflin Co. 1979.

Lois Crisler, *Arctic Wild.* New York, Harper & Row. 1958

Lois Crisler, *Captive Wild.* New York, Harper & Row. 1968.

Rick Bass, *The Ninemile Wolves.* New York, Ballantyne Books. 1992.

Stanley Young & Edward Goldman, *The Wolves Of North America.* Washington DC: The American Wildlife Institute. 1944.

Peter Steinhart, *The Company Of Wolves.* A.A. Knopf. 1985.

Wolves on the Internet

Wild Wolves
www.pbs.org/wgbh/nova/wolves/

Wolf Report
www.poky.srv.net/~jjmm/maugham.html

Reintroduction of the Wolf into the South West U.S.   www.ems.psu.edu/Wolf/

The Ring of the Wolf
www.7threalm.com/wolf/

The Searching Wolf
www.iup.edu/~wolf/wolves.htmlx

The Total Yellowstone Wolf Report
www.yellowstone-natl-park.com/wolf.htm

Wolf Haven International
www.teleport.com/~wnorton/wolf.shtml

Wolf Den
www.tigress.com/wolfden/

Carl Cook Photography
www.halcyon.com/clcook/wolves.htm

The Wolf Education and Research Center
www.wolfcenter.org/

Defenders of Wildlife
www.defenders.org/

The Gray Wolf Web
www.empath.on.ca/clupus/

International Wolf Center
www.wolf.org/

Institute for Environmental Learning
members.aol.com/PugslyPak/index.html

Friends of the Wolf
www.carleton.ca/~sahaddad/wolf.html

North American Wolf Association
www.nawa.org/

Wolves on the Web
www.wolves-on-web.com/

Timber Wolf Information Network
www.timberwolfinformation.org/

Wolf Park
www.wolfsanctuary.org/

Mission: Wolf
www.indra.com/fallline/mw/

Top: Red Wolf at Wild Canid Research Center, MO.

Above: Gray wolf cub.